Handling Relationships

60 Problem-Solving Activities

Steve Bunnell

J. WESTON
WALCH
PUBLISHER
Portland, Maine

User's Guide
to
Walch Reproducible Books

As part of our general effort to provide educational materials which are as practical and economical as possible, we have designated this publication a "reproducible book." The designation means that purchase of the book includes purchase of the right to limited reproduction of all pages on which this symbol appears:

Here is the basic Walch policy: We grant to individual purchasers of this book the right to make sufficient copies of reproducible pages for use by all students of a single teacher. This permission is limited to a single teacher, and does not apply to entire schools or school systems, so institutions purchasing the book should pass the permission on to a single teacher. Copying of the book or its parts for resale is prohibited.

Any questions regarding this policy or requests to purchase further reproduction rights should be addressed to:

Permissions Editor
J. Weston Walch, Publisher
321 Valley Street • P. O. Box 658
Portland, Maine 04104-0658

HM132 .B86 1998
013410966956l
Bunnell, Steve.

Handling relationships :
  60 problem-solving
     c1998.

2007 05 18

1   2   3   4   5   6   7   8   9   10
ISBN 0-8251-3794-2

Printed in the United States of America

Contents

VI. Handling Difficult Situations

To the Teacher

In early adolescence students interact with a wide range of people who are important to them. All of these relationships—with friends, family members, and key adults such as teachers, coaches, and bosses—play an integral part in helping them discover who they are.

Unfortunately, many young people lack the self-confidence and relating skills necessary to make the most of such relationships. They still see situations as outside their control and believe events happen "to" them rather than "because of" them.

The ideas presented throughout these activity sheets are intended to help students recognize the many ways that they can—and do—affect the outcome of their interactions with others. Improving their relating skills can help them to get the most of what *they* want out of their relationships.

Contents

These activity sheets present familiar relationship situations to dramatize problems commonly encountered by young teens. The 60 case studies are organized thematically in six sections.

Section I   *Understanding Who You Are* presents portraits of 10 typical teens and the different problems they encounter in their efforts to relate to others.

Section II   *Communicating with Others* dramatizes the difficulties that arise when teens do not practice healthy communication skills.

Section III   *Getting Along in Groups* focuses on specific problems involved in relating to groups and understanding group dynamics.

Section IV   *Making and Keeping Friendships* dramatizes problems that often occur in close relationships between friends.

Section V   *Working as Part of a Team* presents common relationship problems encountered on the job.

Section VI   *Handling Difficult Situations* includes a final collection of situations that call for "advanced" problem-solving abilities.

Each of these six thematic units is prefaced by a Teacher's Introduction page which describes in greater detail one effective Relationship Strategy that you may choose to share with your students.

Format

Each activity sheet introduces a short case study narrative dramatizing a specific relationship problem to be solved.

This is followed by a short section titled Check Your Understanding, which poses a situation-based question to students to make certain they comprehend the specifics of the case study that they have just read.

Next, in each Case Study Review section, the reader is asked to respond to questions that focus on target issues involved in the problem situation.

In the Ideas to Think About section, students are then presented with concepts intended to help them extract general principles from the specific situation presented.

Last, in the Follow-up section, students are invited to relate the principles they have learned to their own personal experience.

Objectives

Although the activity sheets have been designed for individual student use, it is hoped that you will find them most useful as effective discussion starters. You should work to create a relaxed atmosphere that encourages students to share their individual reactions to the material. Students should enjoy comparing their personal responses to the case study situations after completing each worksheet and feel comfortable sharing their own related personal experiences.

Each of these activity sheets has been designed to develop three related problem-solving skills:

1. **Empathy skills** ask students to name and understand the specific feelings that key characters may be experiencing in each situation.

2. **Analysis skills** ask students to diagnose each conflict by evaluating the motives and needs of key participants.

3. **Problem-solving skills** ask students to offer their own advice for handling each situation. In order to recommend the best solution, they must be able to predict the probable consequences of each choice available.

Ideas for Expanded Use

If you wish to expand upon the themes introduced, I encourage you to use these sheets as the basis for related activities. The following are offered as just a sampling of possible ideas.

Writing Activities

- Ask students to write follow-up scenarios to selected case studies.

- Ask students to create their own case study problems to discuss.

- Ask students to write original stories and poems to explore related relationship problems.

Speech and Drama Activities

- Ask students to role-play case studies and follow-up situations.

- Ask students to write and perform original skits on related themes.

- Ask students to write and perform monologues based on the thoughts and feelings of case study characters.

Media Study Activities

- Ask students to create a class collage from magazine ads related to unit themes.

- Ask students to report on related situations in books, movies, and television programs.

A Final Word

The study of relating skills is obviously of great importance for teens. By learning to take charge of their relationships, they can develop the confidence they need to handle the many complicated situations they face every day—at home, in school, and on the job. By learning to take responsibility for their dealings with others, they will develop a better sense of who they are themselves—and, even more, of who they might become.

Good luck!

I. Understanding Who You Are

Teacher's Introduction

As young people approach adolescence, they can be overwhelmed by the stress of suddenly wondering just *who* they are.

The scenarios in this section dramatize "typical" early teens who respond to new social needs with a variety of ineffective coping strategies, including shyness, showing off, bragging, buying popularity, workaholism, bullying, and even self-bullying.

Such defensive behaviors easily become self-defeating. The characters in these case studies become trapped in their own bad strategies—which turn into bad habits that become increasingly hard to break.

Use these pages to help your students recognize the ineffectiveness of such strategies, and encourage them to explore healthier and more effectual ways to meet these common stressful situations.

A Relationship Strategy to Share

How we think about—and talk to—ourselves can make a big difference in how we feel about ourselves and how we act.

One way to change how we act in difficult situations is to change the ways we think about ourselves—by taking steps to have a more **positive attitude** about ourselves. This takes practice.

1. First, you need to become more aware of the *negative* thoughts that you have about yourself *as you think them*. Listen to yourself more closely when you hear yourself saying things such as, "How could anyone like a person who's as clumsy as I am?" Carry a small notebook to write down such thoughts as you catch yourself thinking them.

2. Next, you need to combat all *untrue* thinking with *true* thinking: "Actually, I'm not *always* clumsy—just when I'm nervous." Most of the time we all really do exaggerate our faults. Write the *truth* beside each negative thought recorded in your notebook.

3. Finally, when you're feeling most relaxed about yourself, practice "Positive Thinking." Choose to review one stressful situation in your day that most often brings up negative thoughts. Picture yourself again in that situation, but this time give yourself a more positive message: "You know, even though I feel a little anxious now, I don't have to be clumsy!"

A better tomorrow really can begin by "rehearsing it" in your imagination today!

Silent Seth

> Some people called Seth "quiet" because he rarely spoke in class. Others called him "stuck-up" because he always sat by himself in the lunchroom, reading a book. Other people called him "a loser" because he went straight home at the end of the day and never joined in any after-school activities.
>
> But *nobody* knew Seth well enough to call him by his real name—"shy."

Check Your Understanding

What was Seth's "problem"?

Case Study Review

1. What different feelings does Seth probably have when he is with his classmates in school?

2. Explain how it is possible that all of Seth's classmates failed to recognize his problem.

3. What suggestions would you give Seth about how to handle his shyness more effectively?

Ideas to Think About

- Shyness is a serious problem when it keeps you from enjoying close relationships with others.

- Many shy people, however, do not realize that *most* people think of themselves as shy—even though they may not recognize shyness in others.

- Fighting shyness is worth the risk. You can learn to feel comfortable with others by taking steps to let them know the *real* you.

  How about trying to get to know better one or two persons who *already* make you feel comfortable? Also, try not to focus on your own discomfort as you make an effort to get to know others better. By "forgetting" yourself, the real you will have a chance to shine through.

Follow-up

Think about situations when shyness kept you from feeling comfortable with others. How did you feel? What strategies did you use to handle the situations?

Metal Mouth

Jenny was horrified to learn that she needed to start wearing braces on her teeth. All of her friends had already outgrown having to wear them.

The day she was fitted, Jenny could hardly eat or sleep, worrying about what people would say when she returned to school. "Everyone will think I'm a total nerd!" she thought.

The next morning at school Jenny saw a boy whom she really liked wave and start walking toward her. She ran into the girls' room and burst into tears.

Check Your Understanding

Why did Jenny run into the bathroom?

Case Study Review

1. What different feelings do you think Jenny probably had about having to wear braces?

2. Why might Jenny feel her friends would think she's a nerd?

3. What advice can you give Jenny about handling her feelings about her new braces?

Ideas to Think About

- It's important for everyone to feel physically attractive. But teenagers often put too much emphasis on the way they look.

- Most people come to learn that their appearance is only one of the ways that they communicate the attractiveness of who they are.

- Feeling self-conscious about aspects of your appearance that cannot be changed is not constructive. Instead, perhaps you can focus on other aspects of your personality you *can* change.

Follow-up

Think about times when you felt self-conscious about your appearance. How did you feel? How did you handle the situations?

Class Clown

Ricardo is always showing off in school and will do almost anything to get attention. He tries to be funny, but sometimes he goes too far.

One day when the class was getting out of control, the teacher said if he heard just one more noise from anyone, everyone would suffer the consequences. Ricardo saw his chance to get a big laugh and started making animal noises in the back of the room.

Nobody was laughing at the class clown, however, when the whole class stayed after school.

Check Your Understanding

What happened to cause the whole class to stay after school?

Case Study Review

1. What different feelings did Ricardo's classmates probably have about his clowning around in the classroom?

2. What do you think Ricardo gets out of always trying to act like the class clown?

3. What other ways can you suggest to Ricardo to meet those same needs?

Ideas to Think About

• Everyone can enjoy being the center of attention, but some people always seem to choose the easy way to be in the spotlight.

• Show-offs who try too hard to win approval from others can end up turning off the very people they hope to please.

• They need to learn that showing off and acting "funny" are not always the best ways to earn the attention and respect of others. One better strategy for getting attention might be to work at becoming really accomplished at an activity that others will respect—such as excelling at a sport or playing a musical instrument.

Follow-up

Think about situations when you tried to get attention by acting foolish. What happened? How did you feel?

Wonder Woman

> When Shana arrived at her new summer camp, she discovered that she was the youngest camper registered.
>
> Soon Shana found herself telling everyone how popular she was in school, how she was president of her class and star of the girl's basketball team—and many other *total* lies.
>
> When the others caught on and began calling her "Wonder Woman" because of all her "accomplishments," Shana didn't know what had gone wrong.

Check Your Understanding

Why did the other campers nickname Shana "Wonder Woman"?

Case Study Review

1. What different emotions was Shana probably feeling when she arrived at her new summer camp?

2. What reasons could explain why she started telling all the lies about herself?

3. What better strategy would you suggest to Shana for handling her uncomfortable situation?

Ideas to Think About

- People who feel anxious about being accepted by others sometimes feel the need to present themselves as different from who they really are.

- Bragging and lying about yourself, however, is usually a sure way to show that you feel less secure about yourself than you try to seem.

- You don't have to be extraordinary to be interesting to others. Take the risk of being yourself, and others will accept the *real* you, too.

Follow-up

Think about situations when you felt the need to distort the truth about yourself in order to make a good impression. How did you feel? What happened?

Big Spender

> Reggie desperately wanted to be popular and was always trying out new schemes to get others to like him.
>
> To win new friends, he would offer to run errands, help with homework, and even lend people his expensive 10-speed. One day when he offered to buy ice cream for anyone who would be his guest, he finally found himself surrounded by a crowd of "friends."
>
> But even then Reggie was puzzled why he still felt lonely.

Check Your Understanding

Why do you think Reggie still feels lonely?

Case Study Review

1. What reasons might explain why Reggie feels so desperate to be popular?

2. Can you explain why Reggie's schemes did not win him the friends he wants?

3. What strategies would you suggest to Reggie for making friends more effectively?

Ideas to Think About

- Many people learn the hard way that friendship cannot be "bought." Friends win the approval of others by earning their respect.

- It's hard to respect others who are so anxious to be accepted that they feel the need to resort to bribes and favors.

- False popularity is rarely satisfying for long. The healthiest friendships are based on an equal exchange of shared interests.

  One better strategy might be to try to become friends with someone who already truly shares a common interest with you.

Follow-up

Think about situations when you have been tempted to "buy" the approval or friendship of others. How did you feel? What happened?

Most Likely to Succeed

Carrie is a top student in her school and a leader in many important school organizations.

She always makes a great show of how "busy" she is and has so many "important" things to do that she never seems to have time for friends. Even if they contact her after school, she is usually too "tired" to accept others' invitations to be with them.

Teachers may give Carrie perfect marks, and parents may call her a model child. But if you ask her classmates, Carrie definitely needs improvement.

Check Your Understanding

Why do you think Carrie's classmates think that she "needs improvement"?

Case Study Review

1. Explain why others react to Carrie the way they do.

2. Sometimes people who work so hard to keep up an image of being "successful" actually are hiding quite different feelings about themselves. What other feelings might Carrie be concealing—from herself and from others—that keep her always too "busy" to have time for friends?

3. What suggestions can you give to Carrie for dealing with all her needs?

Ideas to Think About

- Being successful does not guarantee popularity. In fact, successful people often must work harder to be accepted by others.

- Sometimes people use their success as a mask when they are unsure about how to build successful relationships with others.

- Successful people must avoid getting caught up in their own image and take time to discover—and enjoy—their whole selves.

Follow-up

Think of situations when you have experienced problems in your relationships with others because of success. How did you feel? How did you handle the situations?

Tough Guy

Mort has worked hard to earn his reputation as the school bully. He is always looking for an opportunity to torment others.

When his classmates are playing basketball on the school playground, he grabs the ball and dares anybody to "make him" give it back. When he finally gets tired of being in charge, he just throws the ball in the bushes.

But as he walks away laughing, nobody has any doubts about who the *real* victim is.

Check Your Understanding

Who is the real victim? Why?

Case Study Review

1. Do you think Mort feels as "tough" inside as he tries to appear to others?

2. What do you think Mort is trying to accomplish by bullying his classmates?

3. What more effective ways would you suggest to Mort to get what he really wants?

Ideas to Think About

- Sometimes people mask their real feelings by trying to appear exactly the opposite of how they really feel.

- People who bully others are often the victims of cruelty themselves. Their bullying is a sign of their own troubled life situation.

  The first—and hardest—step of breaking the "bullying habit" is for bullies to admit their own feelings of hurt that cause them to want to hurt others. Talking honestly to a trusted adult can be an important first step in helping them to feel better about themselves.

- Deep down, many bullies find it hard to admit their real need to be accepted by others—often by the very people they choose to victimize.

Follow-up

Think about situations when you may have felt an urge to bully others. How did you feel at the time? What did you do? How did others respond?

If Only . . .

Patty's piano teacher asked her to play in the holiday concert. "If only I played better," she thought—Patty told her teacher "no."

Patty's friends encouraged her to run for class president. "If only I were more confident," she thought—Patty told them "no."

A boy Patty liked asked her to the spring dance. "If only I were prettier," she thought—Patty told him "no."

By always worrying about how she could do better, Patty never got a chance to see how good she really was.

Check Your Understanding

Why did Patty never get a chance to see how good she really was—at anything?

Case Study Review

1. Explain how Patty probably felt when she chose to refuse others' invitations.

2. What do Patty's many excuses suggest about how she might feel about herself?

3. How would you advise Patty to handle her feelings more effectively?

Ideas to Think About

- Some people smother themselves with such high expectations that they never allow themselves to be happy.

- For some people, always looking for ways to be better becomes an excuse to avoid facing challenges.

- Nobody's perfect. It's no crime to accept yourself as you are while working to make yourself the person you want to become.

Follow-up

Think about situations when "perfectionist" thinking caused problems for you. How did you feel? How did you deal with your feelings?

Mr. Cool

Tonight was Tomas's first date with Melinda, the prettiest girl in his class. It had taken him weeks to get up the nerve to ask her out.

When they met at the mall, Tomas was dressed in his older brother's motorcycle jacket, cowboy boots, and sunglasses—all items he never wore regularly at school. For the entire evening, all he did was talk about himself in made-up stories intended to impress her.

For Tomas it was a great date—so he was very confused that whenever he called Melinda after that, she was never at home.

Check Your Understanding

Why does Tomas never find Melinda at home when he calls her?

Case Study Review

1. What different feelings did Tomas probably have about his first date with Melinda? What clues in Tomas's behavior help you guess some of his feelings?

2. What feelings do you think Melinda experienced on her date with Tomas? Why do you think she felt this way?

3. What different choices could Tomas have made to make this a more successful date for both of them? How could Melinda have helped Tomas?

Ideas to Think About

• At times when we feel particularly anxious about being accepted, we tend to believe that we need to act differently from how we usually behave to be accepted by others.

• We may even feel the need to put on a whole new self, believing that our own "regular" identity is not "good enough."

• But others really end up liking us best when we feel most comfortable just "being ourselves."

When you feel tempted to pretend to be someone you are not, admit what's going on—first to yourself and maybe then to others. You may find that others share your feelings!

Follow-up

Think about situations when you felt uncomfortable with others and felt the need to pretend to be someone you were not. How did you feel? Can you think of ways to handle such situations differently?

11   *Handling Relationships*

No Strings

Felicia was an only child. Her father died when she was 10. Two years later, her mother married a man whose wife had died and who had two small children.

Recently, Felicia has started to dress all in black and has asked her friends to call her by the "new" name she has given herself, "Dark Shadow."

Felicia's mother and stepfather have tried to talk to her, but Felicia just answers, "Don't worry about me. I don't need anything from you. You have the younger ones to care for now."

Check Your Understanding

What do you think is prompting Felicia's behavior? Explain your answer.

Case Study Review

1. What feelings do you think Felicia is having about her family and herself? What clues help you guess some of what she might be feeling?

2. Do you believe Felicia when she tells her mother and stepfather, "Don't worry about me." Why or why not? What's really going on?

3. If Felicia had a chance to be totally honest about all her feelings with someone, what feelings do you think that she might share?

Ideas to Think About

- When we start to feel that we are not getting the love we need, we can find ourselves in an extremely painful situation.

- Often, it becomes easier to pretend that our feeling of not belonging "doesn't matter" than to admit our deep hurt and needs to others.

- But it's important in those times *not* to hide behind a mask of not caring and to admit our true feelings.

   Often risking an honest talk with the people whom we feel are hurting us can open up new ways of relating that will heal the hurt. If that is not possible, then talking about feelings with a trusted adult—or even a professional counselor—can keep us from being hurt any more than absolutely necessary.

Follow-up

Think about situations when you felt tempted to deny your need to be loved or accepted rather than to face the pain you were feeling. What choices did you make to handle those feelings? Can you think of ways to handle such situations differently?

II. Communicating with Others

Teacher's Introduction

The years approaching adolescence are a time of increased social interaction. As young people begin the often difficult work of breaking away from dependence on their families, they become increasingly concerned with how they relate to their peer group.

Suddenly, a whole new realm of social stresses comes into play, and a wide variety of new social skills need to be mastered—in closer friendships and dating relationships, as well as in relationships with important adults in their lives.

In the social arena, young teens can easily develop a host of unhealthy patterns in the way they communicate—or more aptly, *don't* communicate—in relationships. Two major themes of the scenarios in this section involve the inability to communicate personal needs effectively and the inability to listen effectively to others.

These extremes—emphasizing one's own self too little *or* too much—can begin to be rectified with the tried-and-true communication strategy described below.

A Relationship Strategy to Share

Many communication problems can be helped by using the communication strategy of employing **"I" messages**. An "I" message is communication that keeps you at the center of your feelings and expression. Using "I" messages can help communication in two valuable ways.

1. First, "I" messages can help to keep disagreements from turning into full-scale arguments. "You" messages put the blame on others and often make them feel defensive.

    For instance, think about how a statement such as "You always are late when we agree to get together!" would make *you* feel.

    When you use an "I" message instead, such as "*I* feel hurt when you keep me waiting," others will react less defensively and be better able to hear your point of view.

2. Second, using "I" messages forces you to be more direct in your communications. Because the emphasis is on letting others know how *you* feel, "I" messages require you to be honest about your real feelings and needs.

    Where it might be tempting to avoid risking a confrontation, an honest statement, such as "I'm feeling angry at you for not calling when you promised," can lead to a helpful discussion about issues that really do need to be addressed.

13

Uhh . . .

> When Lee's cousin Mike came to visit during his winter vacation, Lee took him along to his own school's Valentine's Day dance.
>
> To help Mike have a good time, Lee introduced him to his friend Sharon, knowing that they were both interested in the same sports. He hoped they would like each other.
>
> When Lee returned a few minutes later, however, he was disappointed to see them both silently watching the others dance and not saying a word.

Check Your Understanding

Lee hoped that his cousin Mike and his friend Sharon would enjoy each other. What happened?

Case Study Review

1. What different feelings do you think Mike might have been having in this situation?

2. Why do you think he had trouble making conversation with Sharon?

3. What advice can you suggest to Mike for feeling more comfortable in talking with Sharon?

Ideas to Think About

- Making conversation is not an easy skill to master. It takes practice to learn how to feel confident when meeting new people.

- You can eliminate some self-consciousness, however, by realizing that conversation does not have to be brilliant to be interesting to others.

- The simplest strategies for making conversation are just to start talking about anything—even the weather—and remembering to be yourself.

  Getting a conversation started can be the hardest part of talking to others. One trick is to remember that people often feel most comfortable talking about themselves. Asking a simple question about the person you are talking with often works wonders to get the ball rolling.

Follow-up

Think about times when you had difficulty talking with someone you had just met. How did you feel? What strategies for making conversation worked best for you?

Motor Mouth

> Pete's classmates nicknamed him "Motor Mouth" because he never stops talking. Once he starts, they are lucky to get a word in at all!
>
> He interrupts when others are speaking. He butts into other people's conversations. And he never fails to change the topic around to his most favorite topic—himself.
>
> Worst of all, he has no idea why no one seems to have time to talk to him anymore.

Check Your Understanding

Why do you think no one seems to have time to talk to Pete anymore?

Case Study Review

1. How do Pete's classmates probably feel about his behavior?

2. What does the way Pete acts suggest about how he might really feel about himself?

3. If you were Pete's friend, how would you best try to help him?

Ideas to Think About

- Good conversation is a two-way exchange. Polite listeners don't interrupt, and smart speakers don't selfishly hog the floor.

- A self-centered speaker takes advantage of his or her listeners and selfishly ignores their needs and feelings.

- Good speakers can "read" the signals that listeners give them and know when they have talked too long or are boring their audience.

Follow-up

List some ways that listeners "signal" you to show how they are responding to what you have to say.

Are You Listening?

> Patty had a problem that was bothering her and asked her friend Nadia to meet her after school at their favorite fast-food restaurant so they could talk.
>
> When Nadia arrived in a carefree, chatty mood, Patty tried to hint that she wanted to have a serious conversation, but Nadia didn't catch on. When the boys came in after basketball practice, Nadia pretended to be listening to Patty, but it was obvious that her mind was elsewhere.
>
> Suddenly, Patty got furious and stomped out of the restaurant, without saying another word to her friend.

Check Your Understanding

Why did Patty stomp out of the restaurant without speaking to Nadia?

Case Study Review

1. What emotions did Patty probably feel when she stomped out of the restaurant?

2. How could Nadia have shown that she was a better friend to Patty?

3. How would you advise Patty to handle the situation more effectively next time?

Ideas to Think About

- Sometimes friends need others to listen as they work out thoughts or feelings that are bothering them.

- Good friends make time to listen and show that they care by being there when others need a receptive ear.

- The best listeners listen with full attention and interrupt only to help others expose their ideas or feelings completely.

Most of the time, people are not looking for advice about how to solve their problems. Often the better strategy is to listen quietly and show by focusing your full attention on the speaker that you care about his or her thoughts and feelings.

Follow-up

What do you expect from a friend when you need someone to listen? Are you able to provide the same when your friends need a listener?

Practical Joker

Tony brought a trick hand buzzer to school one day to try out on his friends. He ran into his buddy, Josef, outside the school office.

Ignoring the fact that Josef's appearance suggested that he might not be feeling well, Tony tried to get him to shake hands. Josef refused with a troubled look on his face, but Tony persisted. When Josef refused again, Tony angrily called him a spoilsport and walked away.

Only later did Tony hear the news that the principal had called Josef to the office to tell him that his father had just been taken to the hospital after suffering a heart attack.

Check Your Understanding

Why did Josef refuse to shake hands with Tony outside the principal's office?

Case Study Review

1. What different emotions did Tony probably feel after hearing about Josef's father?

2. What clues did Tony miss that suggested how Josef was really feeling?

3. What advice can you offer to Tony to avoid situations such as this again?

Ideas to Think About

- Tuning in to body-language signals can make anyone a more sensitive listener and better communicator.

- People reveal a lot about how they really feel through nonverbal clues, such as body posture, hand gestures, and facial expressions.

- In fact, many times people's body language will show that they feel exactly the opposite of what their words say.

Follow-up

Make a list of body-language messages that help you recognize how others are really feeling.

What's Wrong with Nancy Now?

> Although Nancy is one of the most talented students in her class, she is also one of the hardest to get along with.
>
> Her mood is never the same. One day she is bright and funny; the next she is moody and mean. Some people suspect that she actually enjoys the attention she gets from her outbursts and temper tantrums.
>
> Although she makes important contributions to many class activities, many of her friends are getting tired of Nancy's being unable to control her emotions.

Check Your Understanding

What might really be going on to cause Nancy's moodiness?

Case Study Review

1. Explain how Nancy's classmates feel about her moodiness.

2. Do you think Nancy behaves the way she does just to get attention? Defend your answer.

3. If Nancy were your friend, what do you think the best way to deal with her would be?

Ideas to Think About

- It's no secret that the body changes of adolescence have a great effect on the emotions you feel. Unexpected mood changes are common.

- However, some people seem to enjoy inflicting their moods on others and make no effort to take control of their emotions.

- Mood swings that are truly uncontrollable may be the sign of a physical illness that requires medical help.

  However, when you find yourself just feeling "blue" or irritable—or full of more energy than you know what to do with—physical exercise can be a great help. Exercise that is vigorous enough to increase your breathing and heart rate can have a lasting, calming effect on your emotions.

Follow-up

Think about times when your moods get in the way of relating well with others. Do you recognize when you are losing control? How do you handle such situations?

What Did I Say?

> As the captain of the cheerleading team, Carly took very seriously her responsibility for teaching new girls the team routines.
>
> One day Carly noticed that Maria seemed a little shaky about some of her moves. Carly asked Maria in front of the others if she had been practicing enough at home.
>
> Maria's face turned very red and she retorted, "I'm doing the best I can!" Then, in a huff, Maria threw down her pom-pom and walked off the practice field.

Check Your Understanding

Why did Maria leave cheerleading practice?

Case Study Review

1. What different emotions could Maria have been feeling when she rushed off the field?

2. Do you think Carly was wrong to criticize Maria? Explain your answer.

3. Would you advise Carly to handle the situation any differently next time?

Ideas to Think About

- Most people find it hard to accept criticism about themselves—even when it may be accurate and meant kindly.

- Expressing criticism is a difficult skill that requires a special sensitivity to others' feelings.

- The best approach involves using tact—the art of seeing the situation from the other person's point of view—*before* you speak.

Follow-up

How do you usually respond when others criticize you? What approaches are easiest to handle? What methods work best for you when you must criticize others?

Name _____ Date _____

Little White Lie

> Philippe tried calling his friend Stan all day on Saturday because they had talked about going fishing together. But there was no answer.
>
> When he finally reached him later that night, Stan said he had been forced to go away unexpectedly with his family.
>
> On Monday, however, Philippe learned that Stan had spent all day Saturday with another friend at a ball game.

Check Your Understanding

What did Philippe discover about Stan's excuse for not being able to go fishing?

Case Study Review

1. What different emotions did Philippe probably feel after finding out Stan had lied to him?

2. What reasons do you think Stan might have had for lying to Philippe?

3. How would you advise Stan to handle the situation differently in the future?

Ideas to Think About

- It is often tempting to avoid a difficult social situation by telling a "white lie."

- Experience usually proves, however, that such lies often get discovered and turn a minor problem into a major one.

- Honesty and directness in relationships may not always seem the easiest approaches, but they usually turn out to be the best.

  When you need to tell others something that might upset them, one good strategy is to start by showing that you care about how your words may affect them. For instance, "Jane, I'm really sorry that what I want to say might make you feel hurt, but I need to be straight with you . . ."

Follow-up

Have you ever handled an awkward situation by telling a "white lie" that backfired? What happened? How could you have handled the situation in other, more effective ways?

Handling Relationships

Good Old Lucy

Lucy tries hard to be a good friend. Her willingness to give time and energy to anyone in need makes her very popular.

But Lucy is beginning to realize that people sometimes take advantage of her good nature. They have come to expect that she will *always* be available when they need a favor and make her feel guilty if she doesn't help out.

Lucy's inability to say "no" to others is becoming a problem, but she doesn't know what to do.

Check Your Understanding

Why is Lucy's inability to say "no" causing problems?

Case Study Review

1. What different feelings might Lucy have in her present situation?

2. Suggest possible reasons why Lucy may find it hard to refuse her friends' requests.

3. How would you advise her to handle her situation more effectively?

Ideas to Think About

- People have a problem with saying "no" for many reasons. But they must realize that saying "no" is always their right.

- Learning to be assertive about how what you will—and will not—do for others is not easy. It takes practice.

   If you have a hard time saying "no" to other people's requests, one effective strategy is to make a rule *never* to give anyone an immediate answer. Just say, "I'll get back to you." Give yourself time—to figure out how you really feel *and* to build your confidence to say "no," if that is what you decide.

- People who clearly communicate who they are and where they stand earn the true respect of others—and themselves.

Follow-up

In what situations do you have trouble being assertive? What strategies do you use to become more effective at communicating your true feelings?

Crutches

After Oleg's skiing accident put him on crutches, his teachers and school friends went out of their way to be nice to him.

But now that he is feeling better, Oleg is embarrassed by all the attention he is still getting and wishes that people would realize that he doesn't need their help anymore.

When his friend Jack offered to carry his books to his next class yesterday, Oleg exploded and told him to stop treating him like a "baby."

Check Your Understanding

Why did Oleg blow up at Jack?

Case Study Review

1. What different feelings was Oleg probably experiencing when he exploded at Jack?

2. Did Jack do anything to deserve Oleg's anger? Explain your answer.

3. What advice would you give Oleg to deal more effectively with his situation?

Ideas to Think About

- Sometimes we expect others to be able to read our minds and know exactly what we want or need at any time.

- In reality, the burden usually falls on us to communicate to those around us what we are thinking and feeling.

- You can't blame others for treating you in a way that you don't like if you have not made the effort to let them know how you really feel.

Follow-up

In what situations in your life could you improve relations by communicating more directly?

Excuse, Please

Kim and Erika took the bus downtown to work on a school research project at the city library. In front of the main entrance stood a small man peering intently at a map of the city.

The man was wearing a headdress and clothing that looked to them like a woman's dress.

"Excuse, please . . ." he began to ask the girls as he approached them. But instead of answering his question, the girls burst into giggles and ran up the library steps, laughing all the way.

Check Your Understanding

Why did Kim and Erika burst into giggles outside the library?

Case Study Review

1. What different feelings do you think Kim and Erika had when they saw the man outside the library?

2. What do you think the man was going to ask Kim and Erika? How do you think he probably felt about the way they treated him?

3. Can you suggest better ways that Kim and Erika could have handled this situation?

Ideas to Think About

• When you come into contact with others who seem different from you, it can be tempting to run away from the situation.

• You may feel any of a variety of possible feelings—awkward, afraid, or even superior.

• But it's important in those times *not* to allow such feelings to keep you from taking advantage of the opportunity to communicate with—or at least help—someone who seems "different" from you.

Often you will find that you have much more in common than you think. Even if you do not speak the same language, it can be possible—and fun—to use hand gestures and facial expressions to share a "conversation."

Follow-up

Think about situations when you felt tempted to run away from communicating with others who seemed "different" from you. What choices did you make to handle those feelings? Can you think of ways to handle such situations differently?

III. Getting Along in Groups

Teacher's Introduction

One very important way that the young person's need for peer acceptance is met is in relationships involving groups.

This section includes a variety of scenarios in which the central character runs into problems relating to groups—either as an outsider or as an insider.

Just as in one-to-one relationships, relating to groups can involve a range of commonly experienced issues. The scenarios in this section include such typical problems as scapegoating, prejudice, peer pressure, divided loyalties, and leadership issues, to name just a few.

One of the central paradoxes of group membership is that belonging to a group can both provide early adolescents with a sense of enhanced personal identity *and* rob them of their all-too-fragile individuality. Young people often hungry to be accepted by peers must find that fine balance that allows them to "remain themselves" while enjoying group acceptance.

A Relationship Strategy to Share

Whether you are outside or inside a group, groups can sometimes try to influence you to think or act in ways that go against your own values. In such situations, you need special skills to stand up to "peer pressure."

The next time you face unwelcome group pressure, try these **assertiveness skills**:

1. Don't react until you're sure of where *you* stand. When group members try to influence you, keep your cool and decide what you believe is best for you. Don't allow others to make your mind up for you.

2. Be direct, firm, and persistent in the way you communicate your point of view. Once you make your position clear, don't let group members try to wear you down.

3. Remember—you don't have to defend your point of view. You have the right to your own decision—without explaining it to anyone.

4. If others still try to convince you to change your mind—leave! Often the best way to deal with continuing group pressure is just to "get out of the heat"—get away from it. If you choose to stay, you run the risk of being swayed by the influence of the group.

The New Kid

> Jamal and his family moved to a new community during the middle of the school year. Even though he is a bit shy, Jamal had managed to make many friends in his previous school.
>
> For the first week in his new neighborhood, Jamal has gone off to school feeling a bit anxious but hoping to make new friends. But all the students already seem to feel comfortable in their own established groups.
>
> At the dinner table last night, Jamal's mother asked how he was liking his new school. Angrily, he told her that all the kids are "snobs" and that he wished that his family had never moved here!

Check Your Understanding

Why do you think Jamal felt angry?

Case Study Review

1. What different feelings is Jamal probably experiencing in his new community?

2. In what ways might Jamal's problem in his new school be his own fault?

3. How would you advise Jamal to handle his situation more effectively?

Ideas to Think About

- It's difficult to break into a community where you are the only new person.

- Being an outsider is not a comfortable feeling. Everyone needs to feel accepted and to sense that they belong.

- Usually, the strategy of just being open, patient, and—most importantly—yourself, will win you acceptance by others.

  Another strategy for successfully breaking into a new crowd is to look for someone else who also seems to be a bit on the "outside." Someone like this might also be feeling lonely and eager to make friends with someone new.

Follow-up

Have you ever experienced being an outsider like Jamal? What problems did you have? What strategies worked best for being accepted?

Members Only

> Suzanne idolized a popular group of girls in her school and desperately wanted them to accept her.
>
> Knowing how Suzanne felt about them, the group pretended to like her while actually making fun of her behind her back. They thought it was funny that she dared think herself good enough for them.
>
> One day in the cafeteria, Suzanne overheard some of the girls in the group saying what they *really* thought of her. Now Suzanne says she'll never trust anyone ever again.

Check Your Understanding

What happened to make Suzanne change her opinion about the girls whom she had admired so much?

Case Study Review

1. What emotions did Suzanne probably feel when she discovered that the group had been making fun of her?

2. What do you think the group got out of making fun of Suzanne?

3. If you were Suzanne's friend, how would you advise her to learn from her bad experience?

Ideas to Think About

- Groups can be cruel in the way they exclude others in order to feel "exclusive" themselves.

- Groups sometimes choose certain victims as scapegoats to tease and bully in order to make themselves more powerful.

- By contrasting themselves with others who are outside the group, members are able to feel more like insiders themselves.

  One possible strategy for dealing with being excluded from a group is to try to talk with a group member whom you feel might be sympathetic to your feelings. Another possible strategy is to start a new group of your own!

Follow-up

Have you ever been the victim of a group's teasing? How did you handle the situation?

Double Dare

> While Tim was visiting his grandparents for the summer, he met a group of kids who invited him to swim at their neighborhood quarry.
>
> When he arrived, all the others were busy diving into the water from the top of the highest rock. Tim was anxious to make a good impression, but he also knew that he could not swim as well as any of his new friends.
>
> When one of the gang dared him to dive like the rest of them, Tim didn't know what to do.

Check Your Understanding

What is the choice that Tim must make in this situation?

Case Study Review

1. What different emotions was Tim probably feeling when he was dared to make the dive?

2. How do you think the other boys would react if Tim did not accept the dare?

3. How would you advise Tim to handle the situation?

Ideas to Think About

- Sometimes it's difficult to know where to draw the line when others pressure you to take risks against your own better judgment.

- You should remember, however, that no one has the right to force you to "prove" yourself in order to win acceptance.

- You—and only you—are the one who must live with the consequences of any risks you decide to take.

  If Tim decides it is not safe for him to dive, one strategy could be simply to tell the truth: "Hey guys, I really don't swim as well as you, and I'm not willing to risk getting hurt." If nobody in the crowd can respect the courage it takes to be straight, then maybe it's time to find a new crowd.

Follow-up

Have you ever been in situations in which you faced peer pressure to take risks that made you uncomfortable? How did you handle them?

Mrs. Willard's Roses

Mrs. Willard is an elderly woman who lives alone. The neighborhood kids have named her "Witch Willard."

One night when they were playing music and talking loudly in front of her house, Mrs. Willard was disturbed by the noise and concerned about her prize flower bed. She called the police to break up the crowd.

The next morning she went outside and found her garden trampled and all of her prize roses broken off at the stem.

Check Your Understanding

Explain what happened to Mrs. Willard's roses—and why.

Case Study Review

1. Explain what feelings probably caused Mrs. Willard to call the police.

2. What feelings do you think led the neighborhood kids to destroy Mrs. Willard's flower garden?

3. Can you suggest better ways for Mrs. Willard *and* the neighborhood kids to handle their feelings?

Ideas to Think About

- Members of a group can be tempted to forget that others outside the group are real people, too.

- Seeing others through the prejudice of stereotypes makes it easier not to take the trouble to understand them.

- Healthy relationships require, however, that group members recognize others as they really are—with needs and feelings just like theirs.

Follow-up

Think about group situations when prejudices have tempted you to treat others unfairly. What made you feel that way? What did you do?

Hotshot

Everybody knows that Larry is the fastest, tallest, and best shooter on the school basketball team. Unfortunately, Larry knows it, too.

His teammates are tired of the way he constantly hogs the ball and tries to make flashy wild shots rather than working more with the team.

To get even, they all agreed to keep the ball away from Larry on the court—and the team hasn't won a game in weeks.

Check Your Understanding

How did the team decide to deal with Larry? What happened?

Case Study Review

1. Explain how Larry's teammates probably feel about his "hotshot" behavior on the court.

2. Can you suggest why Larry behaves as he does?

3. What advice would you give to Larry's teammates about communicating their feelings to him more effectively?

Ideas to Think About

- Team members who begin to think of themselves as better than the rest can present problems for all kinds of groups.

- Cooperation and teamwork are the key to success for any team—on the court or off. No member has the right to expect special status.

- It's up to group members to find healthy ways to communicate how they feel when others forget their responsibilities to the group.

  One good strategy to keep cooperation going is to make sure that the group regularly takes time out to talk about what is going on among themselves. Scheduling time to talk about gripes can work well to keep problems in the group from getting out of hand.

Follow-up

Think about group situations when you have been bothered by others not playing as team players. How did you feel? How did you handle the situations?

Queen Christine

Christine campaigned hard to become President of the Hospitality Committee in charge of planning school dances during the year.

Once elected, she was full of ideas that she shared with her committee members. When it came time for each dance, she always knew just how the decorations should look, what kind of refreshments to serve, and the best music to provide.

What she couldn't explain as well, however, was why her committee of 12 members had dwindled to 2 by the end of the year.

Check Your Understanding

What happened to Christine's committee?

Case Study Review

1. Why do you think so many of the committee members dropped out?

2. What might be some of the reasons why Christine acted the way she did?

3. What advice can you give Christine about how to handle her leadership duties more effectively?

Ideas to Think About

- Being an effective leader is a difficult skill that requires a keen understanding of other people—and yourself.

- Poor leaders enjoy the feeling of having power over others. They become bossy and self-centered.

- In contrast, effective leaders work especially hard to use the ideas and talents of others to accomplish the aims of the group.

Follow-up

From your experience, make a list of the qualities that make people either good leaders or bad leaders.

One of the Gang

Ricardo is a member of his school's champion soccer team. Because they train very hard together and are proud of their record, the team members are very close.

One day one of them suggested that they all shave their heads to show the school how much of a "team" they are. Ricardo was the only one who thought it was a stupid idea and said so.

Now he is the only team member without a shaved head, and the others will hardly speak to him.

Check Your Understanding

Why are Ricardo's team members hardly speaking to him?

Case Study Review

1. What different feelings do you think Ricardo has in his disagreement with his fellow team members?

2. How do you think Ricardo feels being the only team member without a shaved head?

3. How would you advise Ricardo to handle the situation with his teammates now?

Ideas to Think About

• Group members often begin to think, talk, and even look alike. Similarity can be healthy and help a group to feel close.

• Sometimes, however, group members get so close that they feel angry when others do not share their values.

• Conformity in groups is dangerous when it restricts members from thinking and acting responsibly for themselves.

Follow-up

Think of a specific situation in your own life when you faced pressure to conform to group values that you did not agree with. How did you handle the situation?

Stool Pigeon

> Ana was planning to attend Lisa's big party with all her other friends—until she found out that it was to be held secretly while Lisa's parents were away.
>
> Ana was afraid that the party could get out of hand and that someone would get hurt, but she was afraid to tell her friends how she felt.
>
> When they found out that Ana had gone to Lisa's parents behind their backs, however, they were even more angry at their "stool pigeon" friend.

Check Your Understanding

Why were Ana's friends angry with her?

Case Study Review

1. Why do you think Ana did not tell her friends how she felt about Lisa's party?

2. Does Ana deserve to be called a "stool pigeon" by her friends? Defend your answer.

3. How would you have advised Ana to handle the situation more effectively?

Ideas to Think About

- Difficult situations can force individuals to choose between loyalty to their group and loyalty to their own ideas of right and wrong.

- Defending beliefs in the face of group pressure is never easy, but being direct is usually better than trying to avoid a confrontation.

- Groups depend on individuals who are willing to stand up for what they believe—even when they hold unpopular opinions.

Follow-up

Think about situations when you felt unsure about defending unpopular ideas in a group. How did you feel? What did you decide to do?

Runaway Rose

Rose complains to all her friends that her parents are too strict with her. They won't allow her to stay out as late as others her age, or wear certain clothes, or listen to the kind of music that she likes.

But whenever a conflict arises between Rose and her parents over these items, she always reacts very emotionally—yelling, slamming doors, and eventually stomping up to her room.

Her older brother laughs at Rose's inability to sit down calmly with their parents and talk about her feelings. Jokingly, he has nicknamed her "Runaway Rose."

Check Your Understanding

Why has Rose's brother nicknamed her "Runaway Rose"?

Case Study Review

1. What different feelings do you think Rose feels about her parents' strictness? How does she deal with those feelings?

2. Can you guess how Rose's behavior makes her parents feel about her?

3. Can you suggest better strategies for Rose to use in dealing with the conflicts she experiences with her parents?

Ideas to Think About

- When you experience conflict in relationships—especially in relationships such as with parents—it can be very difficult to address disagreements head-on.

- One cause for wanting to run away from conflict may be deep-seated fear that you are powerless in the situation. You don't think that others will really listen to your point of view—*or* you don't want to risk not getting your own way.

- More often than not, however, it turns out better if you try to work out your differences face to face.

    One strategy that you can try during negotiations is to keep a check on your feelings. When parents see you acting more maturely, they may very well start treating you with greater respect, too.

Follow-up

Think about family situations in which you felt that you were being treated unjustly. How did you feel? What choices did you make to handle the situation? Can you think of ways to handle such situations differently?

Gridlock

> The counselors at Camp Pinewood always gathered at the end of each summer season to decide on a gift for the couple who directed the camp.
>
> This year, however, the group was sharply divided. Half of the counselors wanted to give a restaurant gift certificate, while the other half insisted on a new picnic table.
>
> The conversation became more and more heated, and it became clear that neither side was willing to give in. Finally, half of the group just stormed out of the meeting.

Check Your Understanding

What were the counselors disagreeing about?

Case Study Review

1. What different feelings do you think each group had about the gift idea that they were proposing?

2. What different feelings do you think each group had about the fact that the other counselors wouldn't agree to their idea?

3. Can you suggest better strategies for the counselors to deal with their conflict?

Ideas to Think About

- When groups meet to make decisions, often all members do not agree on the same course to take.

- When such conflict occurs, strong feelings can arise in the group and cause a serious split in the unity of the group.

- Perhaps the best strategy for avoiding such a split is suggesting a "time out" in the group when tempers start to get out of hand.

    When emotions cool down, it may be time to suggest that the group begin looking for a compromise solution to its problem.

Follow-up

Think about situations in which you were part of a group decision-making process when a serious conflict arose. What feelings did group members have? What choices did the group make to handle the situation? Can you think of ways to handle such situations differently?

IV. Making and Keeping Friendships

Teacher's Introduction

Just as getting along in groups can pose problems for the early adolescent, so can the complicated issues involved with making and keeping closer, individual friendships.

Here, too, maintaining a sense of oneself while being involved in a relationship can create a host of commonly experienced struggles. This section includes scenarios that involve issues such as loyalty, honesty, negotiating needs, anger, competitiveness, possessiveness, and forgiveness.

These issues can become problematic in all close relationships—same-sex relationships, dating relationships, family relationships, and relationships with significant nonfamily adults, such as teachers, coaches, activity group leaders, etc.

One important lesson your students might learn from these scenarios is recognizing that such problems are a normal part of close relationships and are faced by everyone—and that workable solutions can be learned, too.

A Relationship Strategy to Share

We are all human—everyone makes mistakes. However, in close relationships particularly, it can be very difficult to forgive others when we believe that they have hurt us. Yet forgiveness is often the very element necessary to restore balance to a friendship that is experiencing conflict.

When your friendship is in trouble, try these **Steps to Forgiveness**:

1. Take time to listen to each other. Many times disagreements are the result of simple misunderstandings in which neither party is fully to blame. By taking time to get the "whole picture," the disagreement may be solved.

2. Accept whatever blame is yours—and ask for forgiveness. Many disagreements between friends are kept alive because of each party's inability to take part of the responsibility for the problem. Pride keeps them from admitting error.

3. Be willing to forgive when others ask forgiveness. If you are the hurt party, perhaps the hardest part falls to you—accepting the apology of the other person so that the friendship can be restored. If the hurt is deep, perhaps this step may take some time. It may even be appropriate to ask the other person to make up for the hurt in some way. Ultimately, however, the decision to restore the friendship will rest on you.

Waiting for Danny

> Liam's friend Danny is the neighborhood expert on bicycle repairs.
>
> Yesterday Danny promised Liam that he would come over after school to help him fix his bike. By five o'clock, however, Danny still had not arrived.
>
> This is not the first time that Danny has broken one of his promises, and Liam is beginning to wonder how much of a "friend" Danny really is.

Check Your Understanding

What has happened to cause Liam to doubt his friendship with Danny?

Case Study Review

1. What different feelings do you think Liam had when Danny did not show up as he had promised?

2. Even if Danny had a good reason for not keeping his promise, how could he have shown that he cared about his commitment to his friend?

3. How would you advise Liam to follow up on the situation with Danny?

Ideas to Think About

- Making time for friends and being dependable are important ways of showing that you care about them.

- Being a dependable friend means being there for others when they need you—not just when it's convenient for you.

- Friends prove their friendship by keeping the promises they make. They earn the loyalty of others by being loyal themselves.

Follow-up

Think about situations when friends disappointed you by not being there when you needed them. How did you feel? How did you handle the situations?

What qualities do you expect in a dependable friend? How dependable a friend are you?

Jill's Secret

> One night Jill confided to Phyllis, her very close friend, that she had a crush on a certain boy in their class.
>
> Phyllis solemnly promised Jill to keep her secret completely between themselves.
>
> Jill found out later, however, that Phyllis had called another friend the very same night and told her *everything* that Jill had told Phyllis in strict confidence.

Check Your Understanding

What did Phyllis promise Jill? What happened?

Case Study Review

1. What different emotions did Jill probably feel when she discovered that Phyllis had shared her secret with another friend?

2. What different explanations can you give for why Phyllis shared her friend's secret with someone else?

3. How would you recommend that Jill handle the situation with Phyllis?

Ideas to Think About

- The ability to trust a close friend with your private thoughts and feelings is the sign of a healthy and valued friendship.

- Friends must resist the temptation to betray the confidences of others. There is no room for gossip in friendship.

- Divulging a confidence that has been shared privately between friends is a *serious* violation of that friend's trust in you.

Follow-up

Think about situations when friends have violated confidences that you have shared with them. How did you feel? How did you handle the situations?

Tangles

> Sandra was shopping at the mall when she ran into her good friend, Hilary, just coming out of the new haircutting salon.
>
> Hilary seemed very excited and asked Sandra how she liked the "crazy" hairstyle she had just chosen to surprise her friends.
>
> In truth, Sandra thought it was the ugliest haircut she had ever seen, but to avoid hurting her friend's feelings, she told Hilary that she looked "great."

Check Your Understanding

Why did Sandra respond as she did?

Case Study Review

1. Explain the different feelings Sandra must have had when she saw Hilary's new hairstyle.

2. Would you consider Sandra's response to her friend's question a lie? Defend your answer.

3. How else would you advise Sandra to have handled the situation?

Ideas to Think About

- Being honest is not always easy, especially when it might hurt the feelings of friends you really care about.

- But close friends have a special obligation to be straight with each other—even when it puts them in difficult situations.

- Good friends rely on each other to give honest feedback. Being open and direct is an important way to show that they really care.

Follow-up

Think of situations when you had to choose whether or not to be honest with a close friend. Which approach did you use? What happened?

Name _____ Date _____

Stalemate

> Alec and Barry are best friends, but they have completely opposite taste in films.
>
> Last night they talked about going to the movies downtown, but they ended up in the same old fight. Alec was set on martial arts, and Barry insisted on sci-fi—and neither would give in.
>
> Instead of going to the movies, they ended up going home as they often do—angry.

Check Your Understanding

What happened to Alec and Barry's planned night at the movies?

Case Study Review

1. How do you think Alec and Barry each feel after their disagreement about which movie to see?

2. Do you think Alec and Barry could have avoided their conflict last night?

3. What advice can you give Alec and Barry about how to handle the problem when it arises in the future?

Ideas to Think About

- Even close friends have different attitudes about many things. It's expected that differences of opinion will occur.

- Many head-on conflicts can be solved, however, by using the effective technique of *compromise.*

- When both sides give a little and show that they can be more flexible in their demands, a stalemate can usually be avoided.

  For example, both people can agree to give up some of their demands and meet halfway. Another example of compromise occurs when one person agrees to give in *this* time—in exchange for getting his or her way the *next* time.

Follow-up

Think about conflicts like Alec and Barry's that you have had with friends. Did you use the strategy of compromise to solve them?

    *Handling Relationships*

And the Winner Is . . .

> Robert and Bill have been buddies for a long time and share an active interest in many of the same sports.
>
> At the Spring Sports Awards ceremony at their school, Bill was presented the "Athlete of the Year" trophy—an award that Robert had been expecting to win.
>
> After the ceremony, everyone rushed up to congratulate Bill, but Robert ran in the opposite direction and ducked out the side exit.

Check Your Understanding

What happened to cause Robert to leave the awards ceremony?

Case Study Review

1. What different emotions do you think Robert was probably feeling when he ducked out the side door?

2. Do you think Robert acted like a true friend by avoiding Bill after the awards ceremony? Explain your answer.

3. What advice would you give to Robert about handling his feelings more effectively when he next sees Bill?

Ideas to Think About

- It is expected that close friends will sometimes experience feelings of competitiveness and jealousy toward each other.

- It's sometimes hard, in fact, *not* to envy the abilities or accomplishments of people you like and admire!

- The healthiest way to handle such feelings is to admit them to yourself and realize that others often feel the same way, too.

Follow-up

Think about situations when you have been jealous or envious of friends. How did you handle your emotions?

Scrimmage

Susan and Gail had a small misunderstanding early in the week. Rather than clear the air, however, they let their original disagreement grow way out of proportion.

First, they refused to talk to each other when they met during the school day. Then, they started going out of their way to avoid seeing each other entirely.

Finally, Gail "accidently" tripped Susan in a field hockey scrimmage, and Susan flew into a rage. It took five team members and the coach to separate them.

Check Your Understanding

What happened to Susan and Gail's misunderstanding over the course of the week?

Case Study Review

1. What different emotions were Susan and Gail each probably feeling by the time they began to fight in the field hockey scrimmage?

2. Explain how Susan and Gail could have become so angry with each other over such a small original disagreement.

3. What advice can you give to Gail and Susan about how to deal with their misunderstandings more effectively?

Ideas to Think About

- No close friendship can escape disagreements. It's natural for friends sometimes to feel angry toward each other.

- However, friends need to find healthy ways to express their angry feelings—without resorting to emotional outbursts.

- You *can* learn to express strong feelings effectively while staying in control of yourself at the same time.

  One strategy is to take time alone to "cool down" before sharing your feelings. Another strategy is to make sure you *really* listen to—and understand—the other person's position. Many arguments can be kept small if both participants take time to understand the other's point of view.

Follow-up

Think about situations when you have felt angry at friends. How did you choose to express your feelings? What happened as a result?

Time Out

> Galina's new friend Rebecca is driving her crazy.
>
> She waits for Galina after school to walk home with her. She calls her every night to talk on the phone. And she is constantly inviting her to spend time with her on the weekend.
>
> Galina likes Rebecca, but she doesn't want to be with her *all* the time.
>
> Now when Rebecca suggests getting together, Galina keeps making up excuses to avoid her.

Check Your Understanding

What is the problem that Galina is finding with her new friend Rebecca?

Case Study Review

1. What different emotions does Galina probably feel in her relationship with her new friend Rebecca?

2. What do you think of Galina's latest strategy for dealing with Rebecca's invitations?

3. Can you suggest other more effective ways for Galina to handle the problem?

Ideas to Think About

- Possessive friends often try to monopolize the attentions of others because they feel insecure about being on their own.

- Realistic friends, however, recognize that no one person can be expected to satisfy *all* of another person's interests and needs.

- To keep friendships from becoming stale, smart friends allow each other the chance to enjoy the time to be alone or with others.

  One important strategy for making sure that friends allow each other "space" is to talk about the problem. Avoiding the issue because you are afraid of hurting the other person's feelings just makes the problem worse. Find a time when both friends are relaxed and allow each to talk about his or her feelings.

Follow-up

Think about situations when you have felt the need for more "space" in your relationship with friends. How did you handle the situations?

Randy's Refusal

Randy borrowed one of his friend Pablo's favorite sweatshirts to wear to a party. When Randy returned it, Pablo noticed a small tear in one of the sleeves.

Randy denied knowing anything about the tear and angrily refused to take any of the blame. He said it was more likely that the sweatshirt had been torn *before* he borrowed it—which then made Pablo furious.

The argument lasted for days, with each friend refusing to admit the possibility that he might be the one who was wrong.

Check Your Understanding

What are Randy and Pablo arguing about? Why?

Case Study Review

1. What different feelings do you think Pablo and Randy felt in their argument over the torn sweatshirt?

2. Besides their feelings about the sweatshirt, can you explain other reasons why Pablo and Randy became so angry with each other?

3. How would you advise Randy and Pablo to handle their disagreement more effectively?

Ideas to Think About

• No one likes to admit mistakes. It is never easy to apologize to others, even when you know that you are in the wrong.

• Complicated emotions, such as pride and guilt, make it difficult sometimes even to admit to yourself that you might be to blame.

• Admitting—and forgiving—mistakes, however, usually proves to be the most effective way to resolve a quarrel between friends.

The first step is to take as much time as necessary to discuss the facts of the case. Can the truth be determined? If so, then the second step will be to determine who needs to admit guilt and who needs to forgive. Admitting guilt may be difficult if the facts are not clear, and forgiving may take some time if the offense has been very hurtful.

Follow-up

Think of situations when you have had difficulty admitting you were wrong. How did you feel? How did you handle the situations?

Who Cares . . .

> Raoul and Selena had been dating for seven months. Raoul was very happy in the relationship that they had developed.
>
> That is why he was totally unprepared when Selena told him she wanted to go back to "just being friends" so that each of them could date others, too.
>
> Later, Raoul's best friend told him that he had seen Selena with another guy. The expression on Raoul's face froze, but all he said was "Who cares . . . ."

Check Your Understanding

Why did the look on Raoul's face freeze?

Case Study Review

1. What different feelings do you think Raoul had when Selena told him that she wanted to go back to "just being friends"?

2. What different feelings do you think Raoul had when he heard that Selena had been seen with another guy? How did he choose to deal with those feelings?

3. Do you think Raoul could have dealt with his feelings in a healthier way? Explain your answer. If yes, then describe the better strategy. If no, why was this the best strategy?

Ideas to Think About

- Ending a close relationship can often be a very painful experience. It can be especially difficult if it is not your choice to end the relationship.

- When you feel hurt by someone you have been close to, it can be tempting to deny the strength of your feelings. You may try to pretend—both to yourself and to others—that you have not been affected.

- However, the healthiest way to deal with such situations is *not* to keep those emotions bottled up inside.

  The best strategy is to talk out your feelings with friends whom you trust. Another way to express your most private feelings is to write them out in a personal journal that only you will see.

Follow-up

Think about situations in which someone else has ended a close relationship with you. What feelings did you have? What choices did you make to handle them? Can you think of ways to handle such situations differently?

That's My Girl!

> Connie was a star basketball player on the school team. In the first three quarters of the championship game, Connie made nearly every shot she attempted.
>
> Then, at the start of the fourth quarter, Connie saw her father coming in the door, waving enthusiastically. Though she had asked him not to come, he had made a "sacred promise" to attend every one of her games.
>
> A minute later, Connie stood quietly poised to make a foul shot. Suddenly her father's voice yelled above the rest, "That's my girl!" Connie missed the shot—and didn't make another basket the rest of the game.

Check Your Understanding

What effect did the behavior of Connie's father have on her performance in the game?

Case Study Review

1. What different feelings do you think Connie had when her father yelled, "That's my girl!" during the game?

2. What feelings do you think might have caused Connie's father to yell out when Connie was shooting?

3. What do you think would be the best strategy for Connie to deal with this situation with her father? Defend your answer.

Ideas to Think About

- Do you realize that many parents have a hard time watching their children getting older and becoming less and less dependent on them for their needs?

- When parents experience strong feelings about having to "let go," they sometimes can overreact by becoming overly involved in their children's activities.

- In your relationship with your parents, you can actually help them to "let go" in a number of ways. The best strategy is to keep the channel of communication open.

  Before telling parents about all the ways you do *not* want them to be involved in your life, take time to show them the many ways you *do* still love them, *do* still need them, and *do* want to have a relationship with them.

Follow-up

Think about situations in which your relationship with your parents has suffered because of differing ideas about what you each wanted from the relationship. What feelings did you have? What choices did you make to handle them? Can you think of ways to handle such situations differently?

V. Working as Part of a Team

Teacher's Introduction

Most problems on the job—for young people as well as for adults—are, at their core, relationship problems.

Just as in other relationships, young people who work with others run into a range of predictable, common problems. The scenarios in this section include familiar issues, such as honoring work commitments, sharing the load of job responsibilities, accepting criticism, being assertive, and handling personality conflicts, to name a few.

As in all group dynamics, a special kind of emotional maturity is needed to work with others. The worker must be able to balance commitment to the common task with not allowing others to take advantage of him or her.

When conflicts arise on the job— as well as in other areas of life—teens benefit from having training and experience with the fundamentals of conflict resolution.

A Relationship Strategy to Share

Conflicts are an expected part of living. When individuals with different personalities and points of view are in a relationship, it is normal for disagreements to arise.

Many conflicts in your life, however —both at work and elsewhere—can be reduced or even eliminated by using these principles of **conflict resolution**:

1. Address conflicts early on. If you are aware of a problem in a relationship, fight off the temptation to "sit on it." Usually, problems that you try to ignore don't get solved by waiting—they get worse.

2. Know when—and how—to share your point of view. Once you decide to speak up, it's important to pick a time when everyone concerned is in a relaxed mood and ready to listen. When you speak, try to state your point of view clearly and without extra emotion.

3. Listen carefully to other points of view. It's very easy to get locked in your own view of the situation. Don't fall into the "blaming trap." Try hard to understand what all others involved might be thinking and feeling.

4. Look for win-win solutions together. The best solutions in many conflicts come when all parties involved have an equal share in the process of solving them. Stay open to ideas that others propose as you work together to find the best solution for the problem you share.

Sheila's Day Off

Sheila works as a clerk at a grocery store. Last week another clerk asked Sheila to fill in for her on Saturday so that she could attend a family wedding. Sheila agreed.

On Saturday morning, however, Sheila's cousin arrived unexpectedly from out of state and wanted to spend the day with her.

Sheila called her coworker and told her she was sorry but she couldn't substitute for her after all.

Check Your Understanding

What promise did Sheila make to the other clerk? Did she keep it?

Case Study Review

1. What different emotions did Sheila probably feel when her cousin arrived unexpectedly?

2. Do you think she was justified to do what she did? Defend your answer.

3. Can you suggest other, better ways for Sheila to have handled the situation?

Ideas to Think About

- Workers sometimes find themselves in situations in which they must choose between their work responsibilities and their personal needs.

- Employees must remember, however, that they are part of a working team that depends on them to honor their commitments to the group.

- If you hold a job, be careful not to make promises that you may not be willing to keep. Others at work rely on you to be true to your word.

Follow-up

Think of situations in which you experienced a conflict between a work commitment and a personal desire. Which did you choose? What happened?

Partners

> Martha and Maria decided to go into business together as "Ma-Ma's Baby-sitting Service." They planned to split the jobs—and the profits—50-50.
>
> As it worked out, Maria got stuck with most of the baby-sitting assignments because Martha often had "plans" for Friday and Saturday nights.
>
> When Martha then insisted that Maria stick to their original agreement about sharing the profits, Maria was furious, since she was obviously doing a heavier share of the work.

Check Your Understanding

Why was Maria angry with Martha?

Case Study Review

1. How do you think Maria feels about "partnership" with Martha?

2. Do you think Maria should continue to honor her original agreement with Martha about splitting the profits? Defend your answer.

3. How would you suggest to Martha and Maria that they solve their partnership conflict?

Ideas to Think About

- Conflicts arise in working relationships just as they do in friendships. Partners often have different ideas about the best—and fairest—way to get the job done.

- Working conflicts can usually be solved if those involved are willing to listen to each other's point of view.

- As in conflicts between friends, compromise usually proves to be the best strategy for dealing with disagreements on the job.

  Another important method for avoiding conflicts in working relationships is to make certain that all parties clearly understand the terms of their agreement *before* a problem arises. (For instance, Maria and Martha would not be in conflict now if they had worked out ahead of time how to split the profits if one of them baby-sat more times than the other.)

Follow-up

Think about conflicts that you have experienced in working relationships with others. How did you handle them? Did your solution involve the strategy of compromise?

Short Fuse

Richard enjoys his job at a busy fast-food restaurant. Today, however, he arrived in a bad mood after just hearing that he had not been chosen for the school soccer team.

In angry silence he ignored his fellow workers when they talked to him and scowled at customers when taking their orders.

After spilling a soft drink on an elderly woman and shouting at her to "be more careful," Richard was sent home by the manager without pay—which made him even angrier.

Check Your Understanding

How did Richard's bad mood affect his behavior at work?

Case Study Review

1. What different emotions was Richard probably feeling when he reported to work?

2. Do you think the manager acted fairly in treating Richard as he did? Defend your answer.

3. What strategies would you suggest to Richard to help him avoid the problems he encountered at work today?

Ideas to Think About

- Anger, moodiness, and other strong feelings have little place at work. Successful employees keep control of their emotions on the job.

- Most work situations require courtesy toward others and do not allow employees to take bad feelings out on fellow workers and customers.

- Successful employees bring their best moods to work and find ways to deal with private feelings on their own time.

  One way to release angry feelings is to work them out in exercise, such as jogging or taking a brisk walk. Another way is to talk out angry feelings with someone who cares about you and will listen.

Follow-up

Think about occasions when you brought negative emotions to work situations. What emotions were you feeling? How did you handle them?

Nobody's Perfect

Bonnie was proud of her new job at a fancy delicatessen. In her first week, she worked hard to learn how to make every sandwich on the menu as fast as possible.

That's why she can't understand why her boss still spends so much time watching her and constantly suggesting how she can improve her work.

In fact, Bonnie feels so insulted by her boss's lack of confidence in her that she is ready to quit.

Check Your Understanding

Why is Bonnie ready to quit her job at the delicatessen?

Case Study Review

1. Describe what different emotions Bonnie probably feels in her new job at the delicatessen.

2. Do you think that Bonnie's boss was wrong to criticize her about her work? Defend your answer.

3. What advice can you give to Bonnie about how to handle her boss's criticism?

Ideas to Think About

- Criticism on the job from a boss or supervisor can sometimes seem even more difficult to handle than personal criticism from a close friend.

- Few employees like hearing that their work needs improvement. Pride and defensiveness can make even well-meant criticism hard to accept.

- The best strategy is to try to avoid taking your work criticism too personally and to look for ways to use helpful feedback to improve your job skills.

When you are feeling criticized, take a moment to ask yourself, "Am I hearing any information that could be helpful to me in my job?" It's a fact that employees who care about improving their work and show themselves to be eager learners often get raises and promotions soonest.

Follow-up

Think of situations when you have had difficulty handling criticism on the job. What different emotions did you feel? How did you handle them?

Has Anybody Seen Miguel?

Walter and Miguel both work the afternoon shift at a local supermarket. Their messiest—and least pleasant—chore is cleaning up the bottle return area.

Whenever cleanup time comes, however, Miguel always finds an excuse to be "busy" somewhere else in the store. In fact, he seems to enjoy finding ways to leave Walter stuck with the dirty job.

Walter is tired of cleaning up the bottle area all by himself, but he doesn't know how to handle the situation with Miguel.

Check Your Understanding

Why is Walter having a hard time with Miguel?

Case Study Review

1. What emotions does Walter probably feel about the way Miguel is treating him?

2. What reasons can you suggest to explain why Walter lets Miguel get out of cleaning the bottle area?

3. What strategies can you recommend to Walter to handle the situation with Miguel?

Ideas to Think About

- On any job, there are always workers who seem to take pleasure in avoiding their share of the work.

- Such job "bullies" usually keep taking advantage of others until their victims decide to be assertive and stand up to them.

- Standing up for your rights on the job is not always easy, but it is often a necessary part of working successfully with others.

  The first strategy is usually to try talking directly with the others involved. Tell them how you feel and suggest a solution to the problem. (Sometimes others are not even aware of the problem and are eager to help solve it.) If this strategy doesn't help, then you may need to talk about the problem with a third party—such as your boss—to help you work things out.

Follow-up

Think about occasions when others have tried to take advantage of you in work situations. How did you feel? How did you handle the problem?

Reliable Ruth

At first Ruth felt complimented when her boss, Mr. Morton, asked her to work extra hours in her position as a waitress at his Italian restaurant.

Now, however, it seems that he relies on her to "help out" whenever things gets busy or another employee does not show up for work.

Ruth resents the fact that Mr. Morton seems to expect her to be available whenever he needs her. But somehow she always ends up saying "yes" when he asks her for "just one more special favor."

Check Your Understanding

What problem is Ruth having with Mr. Morton?

Case Study Review

1. What different emotions does Ruth probably feel when Mr. Morton asks her to work extra hours?

2. How would you explain why Ruth always ends up saying "yes" to her boss's requests?

3. How would you advise Ruth to handle the situation with Mr. Morton more effectively?

Ideas to Think About

- It's easy for busy employers to rely on their most dependable workers—and even sometimes come to take advantage of them.

- No employer, however, has the right to ask you to do more than your fair share. You always have the right to say "no."

- It's up to *you* to speak up and share your true feelings. When you keep your opinions to yourself, your employer may not even know that there's a problem.

First of all, make sure ahead of time what your position is and what you want to say. Pick a time to talk about the problem when both you and your employer are relaxed. Try to keep a businesslike tone in your voice (not shy, not angry). Don't agree to any solution that you will not be happy accepting later on.

Follow-up

Think about situations when you have had difficulty saying "no" to an employer's requests. How did you feel? How did you handle the situations?

Handling Relationships

Patrick's Complaint

> Patrick worked on the groundskeeping crew of a nearby resort hotel and looked forward to a big raise after a year on the job.
>
> When the year was up, however, his paycheck remained unchanged, and Patrick was furious! He complained to his family. He complained to his friends. But he *never* complained to Mr. Simpson, his boss and the supervisor of the hotel staff.
>
> After a month of arriving late and slacking off on the job, Patrick finally got fired—giving him another good reason to complain to his family and friends.

Check Your Understanding

What's the *real* cause of Patrick's being fired? Explain your answer.

Case Study Review

1. What emotions did Patrick probably feel when he did not find a raise in his paycheck?

2. What different explanations can you give for why Patrick avoided talking directly to Mr. Simpson, his boss?

3. How would you have advised Patrick to handle the situation more effectively?

Ideas to Think About

- Some people try to solve problems at work by talking about them with everyone *except* the people directly involved.

- Failing to deal with anger and disappointment straightforwardly may cause them to show up in hidden ways that make the problem even worse.

- Although discussing "people" problems face to face may seem difficult, the best solution is usually to communicate your feelings directly.

  To get started, you might try using an opening phrase, such as "Could we talk about a problem I'm having?" or "I'm feeling confused about . . ." or "Could you explain to me why . . ." Stay calm and listen carefully to the answers you receive before you respond.

Follow-up

Think about job situations when you had difficulty communicating your feelings directly. What emotions did you feel? How did you handle the problems?

Quitters Never Win

Lawrence worked hard in his job washing cars for a local auto dealer, but his boss was a difficult person to work for.

No matter how hard Lawrence tried to please him, his boss *always* found something to criticize about Lawrence's work. And when Lawrence tried to talk to his boss about his unreasonable demands, he came away feeling even more frustrated than before.

Finally, after a particularly bad day, Lawrence just threw down his towel in disgust and walked off the lot without even saying good-bye.

Check Your Understanding

What was the problem that caused Lawrence to walk off his job?

Case Study Review

1. What different feelings did Lawrence probably have in his relationship with his difficult boss?

2. Do you think Lawrence was justified in walking off his job? Defend your answer.

3. How would you have advised Lawrence to handle the problem most effectively?

Ideas to Think About

• When employees face serious personality conflicts on the job, sometimes the best strategy may turn out to be choosing to withdraw.

• Employees must learn to recognize "no-win" situations and know when it may be wisest just to walk away from problems that probably cannot be solved.

• It is always important, however, to avoid leaving bad feelings behind. You may need references someday even from a job that did not work out.

If you face a serious personality conflict on the job and you have honestly tried to work it through directly, remember to stay in control. Don't lose your temper, or walk off the job, or try to "get revenge." How others remember the manner in which you leave a job can be as important as the impression you make on your first interview.

Follow-up

Think about occasions when you have had to decide whether to withdraw from a difficult job situation. What did you decide? What factors influenced your decision?

Boss's Pet

Tyrone showed up on the first day of his summer job and discovered that his boss's niece, Risa, had been hired as well.

Tyrone got along with Risa well enough—until it became clear that her uncle was assigning all the fun tasks to Risa and all the boring tasks to him.

For two weeks, Tyrone just put up with the injustice. Then one day, Tyrone exploded—at Risa—so loudly that everyone at the work site could hear!

Check Your Understanding

Why did Tyrone explode at Risa?

Case Study Review

1. What feelings do you think Tyrone had when his boss treated him differently from Risa? How did Tyrone initially choose to deal with those feelings?

2. Do you think that he should have yelled at Risa? Explain your answer.

3. Can you suggest a better strategy for Tyrone to deal with his feelings in this situation?

Ideas to Think About

- Unfortunately, favoritism is a fact of life—on the job and in other kinds of relationships, too.

- Sometimes individuals who show favoritism to others on the job are not even aware that they are doing so. Other times, the favoritism is more intentional.

- Either way, the best strategy in such situations is to talk directly to the persons you believe to be directly at fault. If they have been unaware of their actions, *they* may be willing to change.

  If the favoritism is deliberate, then *you* will be faced with a new set of choices—whether to stay on the job and just live with the injustice or to start looking for a new position.

Follow-up

Think about situations when you were the victim of favoritism. What feelings did you have? What choices did you make to handle the situation? Can you think of ways to handle such situations differently?

Sweet Talk

Anita was very excited when she was hired to work part-time as a clerk in a major department store in her hometown. It was her first "real" job.

On her second day, Mr. Taylor, her supervisor, spent a long time watching her work. Finally, he came up to her with a smile on his face and said, "You know, Anita, you are very pretty . . . ."

Not knowing quite how to react, Anita answered "Thank you." But inside, Mr. Taylor's compliment made her feel very uncomfortable.

Check Your Understanding

Why did Anita feel uncomfortable?

Case Study Review

1. What different feelings do you think Anita had about starting her first "real" job?

2. What different feelings do you think Anita had when her supervisor complimented her?

3. What do you think Anita should do about the situation with Mr. Taylor? Explain your answer.

Ideas to Think About

• Situations such as the one that Anita experienced with her supervisor can be very confusing. When an older person pays attention to you, you may feel both complimented and quite uncomfortable at the same time.

• When another worker pays attention to you on the job in a way that is totally unwelcome, such an action can be called "harassment." Harassment in a workplace is illegal.

• If you believe that you have been harassed at work, your best first strategy is to talk about the situation with an adult whom you trust. With the guidance of that person, you may decide next to talk to someone of higher authority at your place of work.

Follow-up

Have there been situations in your life when attention from someone at work or elsewhere made you feel uncomfortable? What feelings did you have? What choices did you make to handle the situation? Can you think of ways to handle such situations differently?

VI. Handling Difficult Situations

Teacher's Introduction

The scenarios in this last section involve more complex relationship situations that often require greater sensitivity and more mature life skills to handle.

The situations involve such issues as responding to teasing, handling "triangle" problems in a relationship, dealing with money issues, helping a friend in psychological distress, handling emotions such as embarrassment and self-blame, appreciating differences in others, accepting change, and more.

It takes many life experiences—often painful ones—to help an emerging teen grow into a person who has learned how to "roll with the punches" and accept life's inevitable surprises, crises, and disappointments.

An important part of such maturity involves realizing that such events *are,* in fact, a part of life. They happen to everyone. Learning to accept such pain and confusion as "normal" can help mitigate the sting—and perhaps even lead to helping others in their times of need.

A Relationship Strategy to Share

When life gets tough—and it does for everyone at one time or another—we are faced with important choices about how to respond. One tempting choice is to allow ourselves to get stuck in self-pity and anger about how unfairly life has treated us.

This may be a natural response, but after a while it does little to solve our problem. A healthier choice is **learning to let go.**

1. Allow yourself to feel the way you need to feel. Yes, you hurt—whether you are angry, lonely, grieving, or a combination of these. Give yourself time to experience the painful feelings—but don't get stuck there.

2. Learn what you can from the painful situation. Even painful situations can teach valuable lessons. Take time to review the past. Did you contribute in any way to making the situation as painful as it became? What would you do differently if you faced a similar situation in the future?

3. Look for new opportunities. The Chinese word for "crisis" is the same as the word for "opportunity." When any situation changes, new possibilities emerge. Look for the "silver lining" in your "cloud." It's there if you give it attention.

4. Take at least one step in a positive new direction. Keep yourself from staying stuck in the *old* situation by making a conscious choice to explore a *new* possibility— even if you're still feeling the old hurt. Then, just wait for the new possibilities to unfold!

Showdown

William is often the victim of teasing because others know how sensitive he is about being overweight.

The neighborhood kids choose him to pick on because they know how he will react when they call him names like "Fatso" and "Balloon Boy."

Often their teasing makes him so angry that he starts to cry—which of course only makes them tease him more.

Check Your Understanding

How does William react to being teased? What effect does this have on those who tease him?

Case Study Review

1. What different feelings does William probably have when others tease him about being overweight?

2. Do you think William could be partly to blame for the teasing he faces? Defend your answer.

3. How would you advise William to deal with the situation more effectively?

Ideas to Think About

• Bullying is an unavoidable nasty fact of life. All kinds of groups single out victims to tease for many reasons.

• Often, however, victims act in certain ways that make them targets for teasing— and react in ways that encourage the teasing to continue.

• Just showing that you have a sense of humor and trying not to take the teasing so seriously can be an effective first step in handling the problem.

One possible strategy might even be to join in the teasing! Show others that you can laugh at yourself, too: "Yeah, maybe I *am* fat—but that just means there's more of me to like. . . ." (Do you know that many famous stand-up comedians were victims of teasing when they were young?)

Follow-up

Think about situations when you have been bothered by teasing. How did you feel? How did you handle the problem?

Three's a Crowd

Carla has been Sara's best friend for a long time. The two of them have shared many good times together.

Suddenly, Carla has started including Pilar, a new girl in school, in many of the activities that the two friends used to do together. Pilar now often tags along when they go to the movies or run in the park.

Sara tries to be nice to Pilar, but deep down she secretly resents her for butting in.

Check Your Understanding

How is Sara's friendship with Carla being affected by the new girl, Pilar?

Case Study Review

1. What feelings could be involved in Sara's reaction to Carla's new friend, Pilar?

2. Can you suggest explanations for why Carla might want to include Pilar in her activities with Sara?

3. How would you advise Sara to handle the situation most effectively?

Ideas to Think About

- By their very nature "triangle" problems can complicate any relationship.

- Whenever three people—even good friends—do anything together, it's easy for one to end up feeling "left out."

- Rather than wasting time feeling hurt, however, you can face the problem directly by communicating your feelings to those involved.

Follow-up

Think about problems you have experienced with threesomes in relationships. How did you feel? How did you handle the relationship?

Small Change

Jeff ran into his new friends, Pete and Walt, who had just purchased "great" tickets to Saturday's sold-out rock concert.

Without asking, they had also bought a ticket for Jeff—unaware of the fact that he was far less financially well off than they were.

When Pete casually asked Jeff if he could pay them back the $30 tomorrow, Jeff didn't know what to say.

Check Your Understanding

What was the problem that Jeff faced with his new friends, Pete and Walt?

Case Study Review

1. What different feelings did Jeff probably have in the incident with Pete and Walt?

2. Do you think Jeff should pay Pete and Walt the $30? Defend your answer.

3. What advice would you give to Jeff about how to respond to Pete and Walt?

Ideas to Think About

- Money issues often cause problems in relationships where friends do not have equal financial resources at their disposal.

- Friends get into trouble by trying to keep up with others who have greater available resources to spend.

- Avoid such problems by being honest about your own financial means.

  Without revealing more than you feel comfortable sharing, communicate the straight facts to others—without allowing yourself to feel ashamed.

Follow-up

Think about occasions when money issues have caused a conflict between you and others. What emotions were involved? How did you handle the situations?

A Friend in Need

> Karen has been Barbara's best friend since kindergarten. They have come to know each other very well.
>
> Lately, Karen has noticed that Barbara is not acting like herself. She seems distant and withdrawn and much quieter than usual.
>
> When Karen asks if anything is wrong, Barbara just smiles and says "no," but Karen isn't convinced. Deep down she suspects that her friend is keeping a serious problem from her.

Check Your Understanding

Why does Karen suspect that something is not right with Barbara?

Case Study Review

1. What different emotions does Karen probably feel when Barbara tells her that nothing is wrong?

2. If Karen suspects that her friend is really in trouble, would she be justified in going behind her back to get help? Defend your answer.

3. What advice would you give Karen about handling the situation with Barbara?

Ideas to Think About

- Often friends are in the best position to notice when other friends are ill or in trouble.

- Sometimes they must choose to act in their friends' best interests—even when those friends refuse to admit they have a problem.

- If you suspect a friend in trouble needs more help than you can give alone, it may become your duty to ask for assistance from others.

  Asking for help is often the wisest strategy. Think carefully of an adult whom you trust and who would be best to help in the situation: a parent? teacher? school counselor? coach? priest, minister, or rabbi? Then go to this person to ask for help.

Follow-up

Think about situations when you felt responsible for friends whom you suspected were in trouble and would not accept help. How did you feel? How did you handle the situations?

In the Spotlight

One day in the school lunchroom, Fred thought up a crazy stunt to impress Paula, a popular girl in his class.

As he approached her table, he attempted to balance a milk carton on his head. But as he passed by, the carton suddenly tipped over and spilled milk all over Paula and her lunch.

Everyone in the lunchroom laughed at Fred as he clumsily tried to mop up the mess—and Paula ran out of the room without saying a word.

Check Your Understanding

Why do you think Paula ran out of the lunchroom?

Case Study Review

1. How do you think Fred felt when the milk spilled on Paula?

2. What other feelings did he probably have when everyone in the lunchroom started laughing at him?

3. How would you advise Fred to handle the situation now—both with Paula and with others who tease him about the incident?

Ideas to Think About

- Nobody's perfect. All people make mistakes and experience situations that make them feel foolish and embarrassed.

- In truth, the way you handle embarrassing situations reveals more about the real you than the circumstances that cause them to happen.

- When life makes you look foolish, remember your sense of humor. It's a great tool for coping with life's many embarrassing moments.

   Your ability to laugh at—and accept—your own mistakes can be the very best way to handle embarrassing situations. When you feel your face turning red, remind yourself, "Hey, I'm human"—because, you know, *you are*!

Follow-up

Think about occasions when you have been caught in embarrassing situations. How did you feel? How did you handle the situations?

Strike Three

When the school girl's softball team was scheduled to compete for the state championship, Keisha psyched herself up to play her very best.

The game was still close in the last inning, and Keisha came to bat with her team just one run behind. Knowing that one hit could save the game, she confidently approached the plate—and struck out.

After the game and even two weeks later, Keisha wouldn't speak to any of her teammates. No one could convince her to stop blaming herself for losing the state championship for her team.

Check Your Understanding

Why is Keisha not speaking to the girls on her softball team?

Case Study Review

1. Describe what different emotions Keisha probably felt after striking out in the championship game.

2. Do you think she is right to feel responsible for losing the state championship for her team? Explain your answer.

3. If you were one of Keisha's teammates, how could you help her to handle her feelings more effectively?

Ideas to Think About

- Learning to live with failure is sometimes hard. It's easy to feel shame when you feel you have disappointed others.

- But people who do not easily accept their mistakes must realize that no one can expect you to be a winner *all* the time—not even yourself.

- Sharing your pain and disappointment with others is a good way to put failure behind you and get on with working toward future successes.

Follow-up

Think about times when you have experienced trouble dealing with failure and disappointment. How did you choose to handle your feelings?

Moving On

Alan and Mark have shared a lot of experiences together and have been best friends for a long time.

When school started this year, however, Mark sensed that his relationship with Alan had changed. They don't talk as easily as they once did, and Alan seems more interested in spending time with new friends than with him.

When Mark sees Alan having a good time with others, he is ashamed to find himself almost hating the person who used to be his best friend.

Check Your Understanding

How does Mark react when he sees Alan having a good time with others? How does he feel about his own reaction?

Case Study Review

1. What are some of the different emotions that Mark is probably feeling about the change in Alan's feelings toward him?

2. Do you think that Mark actually "hates" his former best friend? Defend your answer.

3. In what ways would you advise Mark to deal with the strong emotions he is feeling?

Ideas to Think About

- It's a sad fact of life that relationships sometimes change and friends move unexpectedly in different directions.

- Friends who experience a loss can be tempted to let the hurt feelings make them forget the positive feelings they originally held.

- Accepting loss and change as an inevitable part of all relationships allows you to move on more easily to develop satisfying new ones.

Follow-up

Think about occasions when you have had difficulty accepting change in your relationships. How did you handle your feelings?

  Handling Relationships

Wanna Dance?

> Without a doubt, Dana was the most popular girl in her grade. She was smart, pretty, and a star athlete, too.
>
> Randy was a different story altogether. His clothes never seemed to fit, he was slow and clumsy, and he always seemed awkward in front of others—especially girls.
>
> That's why all Dana's friends were "horrified" when Randy walked up to Dana at the Valentine's Day dance and awkwardly asked her if she would like to dance.

Check Your Understanding

What happened at the dance to cause Dana's friends to be horrified?

Case Study Review

1. A popular girl like Dana could respond to Randy's invitation to dance with many different feelings. Describe some emotions that Dana might have felt in this situation.

2. Do you think Dana's friends were right to feel "horrified" when Randy asked her to dance? Defend your answer.

3. How would you have advised Dana to respond to Randy's invitation?

Ideas to Think About

- Of all the skills necessary to help build healthy relationships, the most important by far is the ability to be kind.

- Each day presents new opportunities for everyone to choose to exercise kindness toward others.

- By choosing to be kind, you give the very best of yourself, and your example encourages others to give the best of themselves, too.

Follow-up

Think about difficult situations when you have been faced with the choice of being kind to others. How did you feel? What did you decide to do?

Where's Mr. Harris?

José was a very shy student who had few friends. But, when the new school guidance counselor was hired, everyone was surprised to see how easily José talked with him.

Mr. Harris was young and was a very good listener, so many students liked him. Halfway into the year, however, Mr. Harris was fired, without warning, for using drugs.

The other students were surprised, but José was devastated. In fact, he barely spoke to anyone at school for the rest of the year.

Check Your Understanding

Why do you think José was so quiet for the rest of the year?

Case Study Review

1. What different emotions do you think José felt when he first developed a friendship with Mr. Harris?

2. What different feelings do you think José experienced when Mr. Harris was fired without warning?

3. How did José deal with his disappointment? Could you suggest any healthier strategies for him to deal with his disappointment?

Ideas to Think About

- It's very painful to have any person whom you seriously care about disappoint you.

- You can end up with a mixture of strong feelings—angry, sad, hurt, and very confused. It's tempting at times like these just to withdraw and keep your pain to yourself.

- But, in fact, this is a particularly difficult time, and you need to share your hurt with others who care about you.

  Friends your own age are a place to start. But if the hurt is really deep, it's probably better to turn to an adult whom you trust—a parent, teacher, or neighbor, for example—who has the experience to help you.

Follow-up

Think about situations in your life when you were seriously disappointed by someone you trusted. How did you handle your painful feelings? Can you think of ways to handle such situations differently?

How's Francie Doing?

> The whole school was shocked when Francie's grandmother and younger cousin were killed in an auto accident.
>
> Afterwards, Francie was out of school for more than a week. On the day she returned, she seemed very quiet—and everyone she came in contact with seemed to turn quiet, too.
>
> The truth was, in fact, that everybody in school was talking *about* Francie and the terrible accident, but hardly anyone knew what to say *to* Francie.

Check Your Understanding

Why do you think the students were acting differently toward Francie?

Case Study Review

1. What different emotions do you think Francie was feeling on her first day back to school?

2. What different feelings do you think the other students experienced when they saw Francie?

3. Do you think the other students made the correct choice in how they treated her on her first day back? Explain your answer. If not, can you suggest better strategies for them to deal with her and their own feelings?

Ideas to Think About

- It can be very difficult to know what to say to friends who have suffered a painful loss.

- You feel confused about the best way to comfort them—and even feel tempted to avoid them, fearing you might cause them more pain by talking directly about their loss.

- The best strategy, however, usually turns out to be to acknowledge the loss briefly to them. People who are grieving need to know that friends are caring about them.

  After this, however, take your next cue from them. Listen carefully to how they react to figure out how you can best help them—run errands, cook a meal, or maybe just offer to listen as they talk about their pain.

Follow-up

Think about situations in which you had to deal with someone who had suffered a serious loss. What feelings did you have? What choices did you make to handle the situation? Can you think of ways to handle such situations differently?

Share Your Bright Ideas with Us!

We want to hear from you! Your valuable comments and suggestions will help us meet your current and future classroom needs.

Your name_____Date_____

School name_____Phone_____

School address_____

Grade level taught_____Subject area(s) taught_____Average class size_____

Where did you purchase this publication?_____

Was your salesperson knowledgeable about this product?   Yes_____   No_____

What monies were used to purchase this product?

____School supplemental budget   ____Federal/state funding   ____Personal

Please "grade" this Walch publication according to the following criteria:

Quality of service you received when purchasing ....A   B   C   D   F
Ease of use..A   B   C   D   F
Quality of content..A   B   C   D   F
Page layout ....A   B   C   D   F
Organization of material ....A   B   C   D   F
Suitability for grade level ....A   B   C   D   F
Instructional value..A   B   C   D   F

COMMENTS:_____

_____

What specific supplemental materials would help you meet your current—or future—instructional needs?

_____

Have you used other Walch publications? If so, which ones?_____

May we use your comments in upcoming communications?   ____Yes   ____No

Please **FAX** this completed form to **207-772-3105**, or mail it to:

Product Development, J.Weston Walch, Publisher, P.O. Box 658, Portland, ME 04104-0658

We will send you a **FREE GIFT** as our way of thanking you for your feedback. **THANK YOU!**